SAFARI READERS
2
BOOK STAGE

Sea Turtles

SAFARI
READERS

Tristan Walters

For Billy & Phoebe

- the original Safari Readers!

www.safarireaders.com

Written & Designed by Tristan Walters

Acknowledgements [Abbreviation Key: FVM—FreeVectorMaps.com; SS – Shutterstock.com]

Cover (background), Yulin Studzinska/SS; Cover (middle), Willyam Bradberry/SS; 1, Rich Carey/SS; 2-3, Shane Myers/SS; 4, Pei Chung Davy/SS; 5 (left), Janos Rautonen/SS; 5 (middle left), Maridav/SS; 5 (middle right), Adhi Rachdian/SS; 5 (bottom), Rich Carey/SS; 6-7 (background), Joakant/PX; 8, Andrey Armyagov/SS; 9, FreeVectorMaps/FVM; 10-11 (background), Vitaly Korovin/SS; 11 (sea krait), Rich Carey/SS; 12, Isabelle Kuehn/SS; 13 (top right, top left, bottom middle), Maquiladona/SS; 13 (bottom left), Joost Van Uffelen/SS; 14-15, Stephanie Rousseau/SS; 16, Chai Seamaker/SS; 18, StockSnap/PX; 19, Kazakova Maryia/SS; 19, gibalos/SS; 20-21, Kathayut Kongmanee/SS; 21 (top), Julio Salgado/SS; 21 (bottom), Pigrox/SS; 22, Willyam Bradberry/SS; 25, Iva Villi/SS; 26, Blue Orange Studio/SS; 28 (4th down), Shane Myers/SS; Animation Images (Back, 5, 7, 9-10, 15, 19, 23-28), Memo Angeles/SS.

Contents

What is a sea turtle?

Did you know?
The first sea turtles lived over 200 million years ago.

4

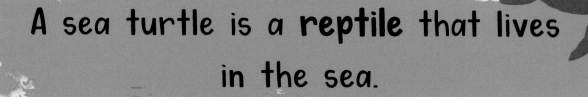

A sea turtle is a **reptile** that lives in the sea.

saltwater crocodile

marine iguana

Komodo dragon

sea snake

What other **reptiles** can be found in the sea?

Check out the words in **bold** in our glossary on the back page.

5

What does a sea turtle look like?

SEA TURTLE

 SCIENTIFIC NAME
Chelonia

 SIZE
Up to 2m long

 WEIGHT
Up to 700 kg

 SPEED
30 km per hour

 AGE
Up to 100 years

back flipper

short tail

front flipper

Where do sea turtles live?

Did you know?
Some turtles **migrate** across whole oceans so that they can feed or nest.

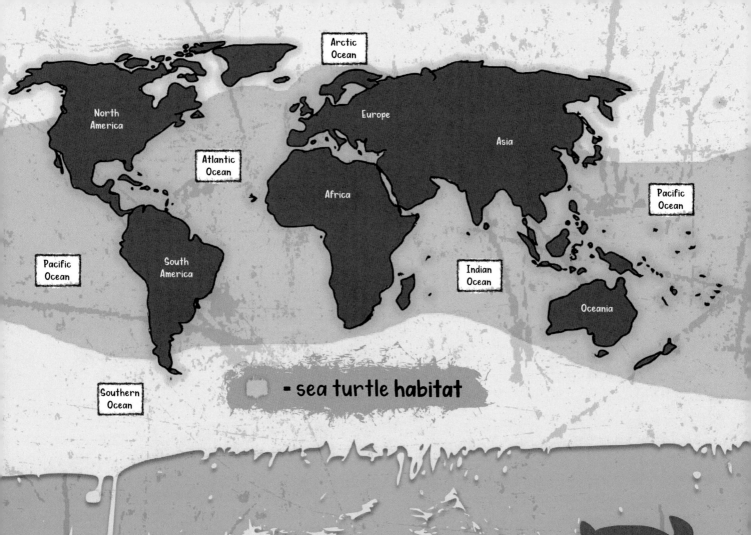

- = sea turtle habitat

Sea turtles spend most of their lives swimming in the sea.

9

Where do sea turtles live?

NINGALOO REEF
WESTERN AUSTRALIA

 LOCATION
Australia, Oceania

 HABITAT
Coral reef and
coastal lagoon

 SIZE
5,000 km²

black-tip
reef shark

blue tang

clownfish

hermit crab

What types of sea turtle are there?

hawksbill

Did you know?
Six of the seven kinds of sea turtle are now **endangered**.

TYPES OF SEA TURTLE

green

loggerhead

leatherback

flatback

Kemp's ridley

Olive's ridley

There are seven kinds of sea turtle living across the world.

How big can sea turtles grow?

GIANT TURTLE

7 FEET

leatherback turtle

human

The leatherback is the biggest turtle and can grow up to seven feet long.

What do sea turtles eat?

Did you know?
Sea turtles have no teeth but have a sharp beak to feed with.

SEA TURTLE MENU

crab

sea grass

shrimp

Can you spot what the turtle is feeding on?

Some sea turtles eat animals and others just feed on plants.

Where do sea turtles lay their eggs?

Did you know?
Sea turtles return to the beach where they were born to lay their eggs.

Mother sea turtles come onto land to dig a nest and lay their eggs.

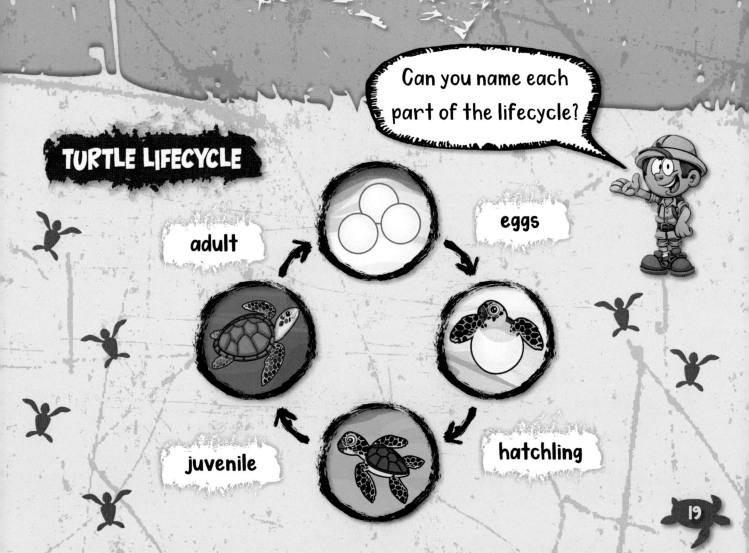

Can you name each part of the lifecycle?

TURTLE LIFECYCLE

adult

eggs

juvenile

hatchling

Did you know?
Up to 200 sea turtles can hatch from one nest!

hatching from the nest

crawling along the beach

reaching the sea

After two months, the sea turtles hatch and find their way to the sea.

Why are sea turtles in trouble?

Did you know?
Lots of sea animals eat plastic as they think it is food.

Extinct	Extinct in the Wild	Critically Endangered	Endangered	Vulnerable	Near Threatened	Least Concern

CONSERVATION STATUS

13 MILLION
tons of plastic goes into the sea every year!

Over

50%

of sea turtles have had plastic found in their stomachs.

How can we stop plastic going in the sea?

Lots of sea turtles are killed by nets, plastic and rubbish in the sea.

Sea Turtle Puzzle

PUZZLE 1

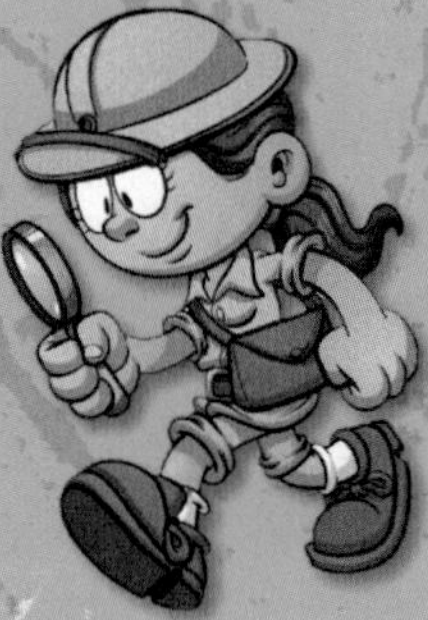

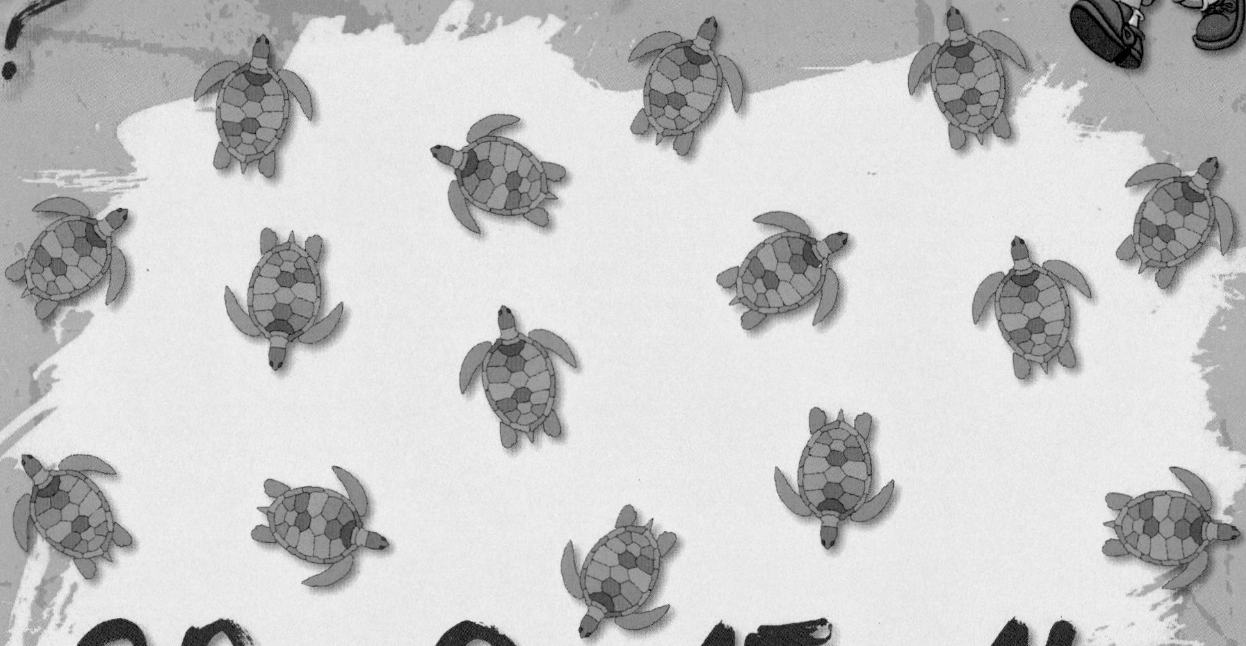

20 9 15 14

Safari Readers

The 'Safari Readers' books are specially designed to help children learn to read. Based on leading teaching practice, this series enables children to develop a range of reading skills and create a love of reading and language through wild and exciting topics.

Enjoy the ride!

SAFARI READERS

Reading is fun! These books are best enjoyed when reading together.

The smaller text can be read by whoever is supporting the child.

The larger text is for the child to read.

There is a book for all our 'Safari Readers' out there.

Why not join 'Safari Sam' and 'Safari Suzy' and explore the other books

we have in the series!

STAGE 1

Cheetahs ☐ Flamingos ☐ Wolves ☐ Giraffes ☐ Dolphins ☐

STAGE 2

Sea Turtles ✓ Tigers ☐ Elephants ☐ Polar Bears ☐ Gorillas ☐

STAGE 3

Sharks ☐ Lions ☐ Penguins ☐ Snakes ☐ Monkeys ☐

For more information check out our website:

WWW.SAFARIREADERS.COM

Glossary

Can you remember all of the new words we have learnt?

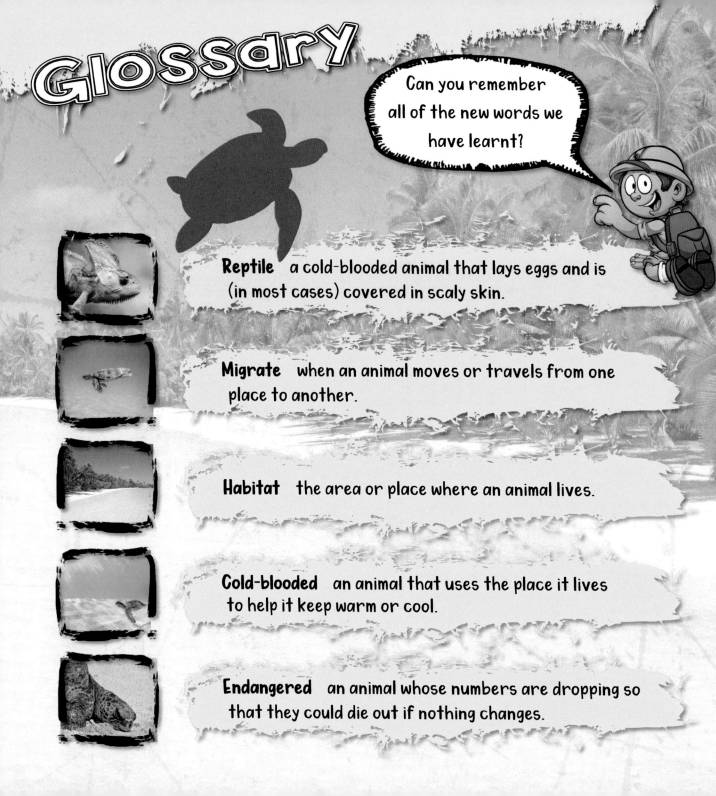

Reptile   a cold-blooded animal that lays eggs and is (in most cases) covered in scaly skin.

Migrate   when an animal moves or travels from one place to another.

Habitat   the area or place where an animal lives.

Cold-blooded   an animal that uses the place it lives to help it keep warm or cool.

Endangered   an animal whose numbers are dropping so that they could die out if nothing changes.

Made in the USA
Coppell, TX
08 March 2020